scars like constellations

cristie robbins

scars like constellations

@ 2025 Cristie Robbins

Independently Published
Printed in the United States of America

ISBN: 979-8-9927745-1-1

Cover design by Cristie Robbins

This is a work of poetry. Any similarities to actual persons, living or dead, or real events is purely coincidental unless stated otherwise by the author.

For my brother, whose absence shaped me,
and for my children, who remind me why I rise.

acknowledgments

To my mother and sister, whose unconditional and fearless love have shown me the depths of my own ability. You have held me through every season of my life, never wavering, always believing in me—even when I struggled to believe in myself.

To my husband, who encourages me to write, to grow, to heal. Your complete acceptance of my journey has given me the space to become everything I was always meant to be.

To my children, who are my greatest teachers. You have given me purpose, strength, and more love than I ever knew was possible. You remind me, every day, why I rise.

To every reader who finds themselves in these pages—may you know you are not alone.

introduction

I did not set out to write these poems.
I set out to survive.

To make sense of grief that never left.
To unravel trauma that lived in my bones.
To name the ghosts that lingered
long after I should have been free of them.

Some of these poems were written
from the wreckage—
when I did not yet know
there was a way out.

Some were written after I crawled my way forward,
after I unlearned the lies
that had been whispered to me since childhood—
that love should hurt,
that silence was safety,
that survival was enough.

This is not just a collection of poetry.
It is a record of breaking,
of haunting,
of unlearning,
of becoming,
of rising.

And if you have ever felt lost,
if you have ever carried wounds
that no one else could see,
if you are still searching for the way forward—

This book is for you.

contents

acknowledgments   i

introduction   ii

the breaking   1

   pockets full of ghosts   2

   the weight of what's left behind   3

   splintered   4

   the things we clean   5

   unsaid   6

   the teeth on the floor   7

   aloneness   8

   the question that never leaves   10

   what the body remembers   11

   precious memories   12

   night   15

   some things do not heal   17

   a house that was never home   18

   madness   19

   inheritance   20

   the hardest truth   21

the haunting   23

   the ghost between us   24

   where do you put the love that has nowhere to go?   25

   echoes   26

   the weight of air   27

i don't know when it happened   28
when i met her   30
fractured time   32
splinters   33
permission   34
the exercise i could not complete   35
i became   36
the things he said   38
still looking   39
the echo stops with me   40
some days i want to disappear   41
no one saves you   43
the version of me that loved you   44
the door i closed   45

the unlearning   47
the ghosts i carry   48
the art of leaving   49
penny   50
too tired   53
the list   55
the dirty things we do   56
what i was supposed to be   58
the body remembers   59
the man in the mirror   60
repetition   62

what i will not pass down   63
she is still in the fire   64
what they never told
you about survival   66
i have never been soft   67
a war without weapons   68
the things i wish i could tell her   69

the becoming   71
    unapologetic   72
    do not call me small   74
    sunrise   76
    a woman like me   77
    the weight of motherhood   78
    soft love   79
    becoming   80
    twitch   81
    the kind of woman i have become   82
    set me on fire   83
    you wouldn't recognize me now   84
    not a good girl   85
    the woman who disappeared   86
    the body keeps it all   88
    learning softness   89

the rising   91

    the second life   92

    inheritance of light   93

    unfinished   94

    between the breaths   95

    hunger   96

    unbecoming   97

    they are not mine   98

    fingertip prayers   100

    the parts i keep   101

    i did not die with it   102

    breaking the cycle   103

    becoming the phoenix   104

    i will not be the quiet woman   105

    i found myself in ireland   106

    the kind of love that does not hurt   108

    what they don't tell you about survival   109

    scars like constellations   111

about the author   113

the
breaking

pockets full of ghosts

I have seen addiction wear my last name.

It sat at my father's table,
spilled from his trembling hands,
curled around his body at night,
a ghost he could not lay to rest.

His pockets were full
of orange bottles
that whispered his name,
their voices softer
than his demons.

I have seen addiction in my son's restless eyes,
the way he chases
a high that has no name,
the way he runs before the silence
can catch him.

How do you love someone
who is always slipping
through your fingers?

How do you break a cycle
when the road ahead of you
looks just like the one behind?

Some nights, I wonder
if hunger is something
we inherit.

the weight of
what's left behind

I did not know grief
could be so heavy.

That it could sit in my bones
long after the funeral,
long after the flowers wilted,
long after the world decided
it was time to move on.

But I am still here,
carrying the weight
of everything you left behind—

The things you touched last.
The words you never said.
The life you should still be living.

And some days,
it is not sorrow
that I feel most.

It is the exhaustion
of holding onto
someone
who is no longer here.

splintered

The house still smells of rain
from the night the world caved in.
Shattered glass, a door left swinging,
the air thick with words unsaid.

I press my fingers to the walls,
feel the pulse of the past
beating beneath the paint.

Some wounds do not close.
They linger, splintered beneath the skin,
a silent ache,
a ghost that does not know
it is dead.

the things we clean

Grief is not just sorrow—
it is scrubbing blood from walls,
lifting shattered bone from the floor,
holding a life in your hands
long after it has ended.

We did not get the luxury
of leaving it to strangers.
No men in white suits,
no faceless crew
to carry it away.

It was us.
It was family.

And so, we did what families do.
We cleaned.
We gathered the pieces.
We made the house whole again,
as if we could not see
the emptiness it now held.

But no amount of bleach
can erase what the walls remember.

No matter how hard we scrub,
the ghost of him
does not wash away.

unsaid

The things I never told you
hang in the air like dust—
suspended, weightless,
waiting to settle.

I should have said I love you
louder,
held on longer,
made you believe
you were more than your darkness.

Now, silence carries your name.
Now, I whisper to ghosts.

the teeth on the floor

I laid down in the room
where he left us,
pressed my cheek to the floor,
as if I could listen for something—
his voice, his breath,
a sign that this was all a mistake.

I should not have looked.

But grief is cruel,
and curiosity is its sharpest blade.

Something glinted beneath the couch,
small, white,
like lost pearls scattered in the dust.

Teeth.
Skull.

He was everywhere
and nowhere.

And I—
I was left holding pieces
of what could never be put back together.

aloneness

Why didn't I cry?

In my 20's, I was
Numbness.
Aloneness.
I was a ghost within my
existence.

I didn't cry.
Ever.
Nothing penetrated the
armor I held to
so tightly.

Why was I born, daddy?
I don't know yet.

In my 30's, I was
Anger.
Aloneness.
I was a ghost within my
motherhood.
My children felt it.
I felt very little.

I still didn't cry.
I raged.
Nothing penetrated the
armor I held to
so tightly.

Why was I born, daddy?
I don't know yet.

In my 40's,
I can't stop crying.
I can't stop feeling
everything.
Life is so delicate
and vulnerable.

Why wasn't I ever strong enough
to see beyond my
Aloneness?

the question that never leaves

I still wonder
if you regretted it
the moment after.

If you reached for the air,
if you wished for more time,
if you tried to take it back
but your body had already moved forward
without you.

I do not know what you saw
in those final seconds.

Did the world narrow to a pinprick?
Did it open into something vast?
Did you hear our voices,
or only silence?

There is no answer.
Only this question
that echoes
inside the spaces
where you used to be.

what the body remembers

It does not matter
how many years have passed.

The body keeps count.

It remembers the slammed doors,
the words that cut deeper than fists,
the way fear curled itself
around your ribs
until breathing became
something you had to earn.

It remembers the nights
you braced for a battle
that never came—
the ones where silence
was the sharper weapon.

The mind forgets,
forgives,
rewrites the story
into something survivable.

But the body—
the body still flinches
when the wind sounds
like footsteps.

precious memories

We stood before my brother's coffin,
overwhelmed, numbed,
staring into the impossible.

"Dell has killed himself."

The words echoed in my skull,
a sentence that did not belong
in our family's story.

A voice rose from the back of the room,
haunting, hollow, whole—

"Precious memories, unseen angels,
sent from somewhere to my soul..."

My mother stood,
slow, fragile,
as if her body knew something
her heart refused to accept.

"How they linger, ever near me,
and the sacred past unfold..."

She knelt before his coffin,
threw her hands into the air.
Her lips moved, but I could only hear
the sound of her breaking.

Praying.
Pleading.
Wishing his life had been softer.
Wishing his death had never come.

"Precious memories, how they linger,
how they ever flood my soul..."

I looked down.
Grief sat heavy in my throat,
thicker than air,
thicker than prayer.

"As I travel on life's pathway,
know not what the years may hold..."

But I knew.
I knew what this year had held.
I knew what my hands had touched,
what my knees had pressed into.

I knew the weight of his absence.

"As I ponder, hope grows fonder,
precious memories flood my soul..."

My mother rose again,
floating back to her seat,
a ghost of the woman
who once believed prayer
was enough.

"In the stillness of the midnight,
precious, sacred scenes unfold..."

But I knew what that midnight held.
I knew the stains that do not wash away.

His blood on the walls.
The fragments of his body
left behind.
My hands on the floor,
searching,
breaking,
unable to undo what had been done.

"Precious memories, how they linger,
how they ever flood my soul..."

night

I watched his bloodied body carried into
our living room from the remains of an attempted end
that failed. His car destroyed but his heart still intact.

From behind my teenage eyes, I saw him battered and bruised –
being wrapped and healed, and when he finally awoke
he asked with his pained look, "Am I still
alive?"

In 1998, my mother told me – he ran off
into the night with promises of the rope, the gun,
the gas left on, the slash of a blade. But the heart did not
stop, the blood wouldn't leak, and in an all-too familiar room
he asked as he cried, "Am I still
alive?"

Possibly next
time dearest brother, the desired peace will be found.
I know that now.
The seasons of night hold the air which grasps you
too tightly during this journey.

Until everything finally stops, your
face twitches with a lamenting wind for
death, a beautifully colored candy held just beyond your grasp,
slipping off your fingertips – so tender and promising you can almost
feel.

Why try to encapsulate life with the soiled hands of love when
nothing ever happens but the
night?

some things do not heal

They say time heals.
But they do not tell you
that some wounds
do not close.

Some wounds
become part of you.
Soft scars beneath your skin,
ghosts in the spaces
between your ribs.

I do not bleed anymore,
but I am not whole.

And maybe
I never will be.

a house that was never home

I grew up in a house
where love came with conditions,
where silence held its breath
and walls swallowed apologies
that were never spoken.

A house is not a home
just because people live inside it.
Not when you learn to walk quietly,
not when you brace for words
sharper than fists,
not when you carry its weight
long after you leave.

I have spent years
unlearning the lessons of that place.
I have spent years
teaching myself
that love does not
have to hurt.

madness

I have dipped my hands into the madness of discontent,
and with the drops still falling off
my fingertips, I beg you
to see me.

Turn out the lights, maybe then...

Then you can see the passion in my touch, the need
for your honesty, and a longing for tomorrow's season.

See me for the wonder that lies on my chest,
the desire that whispers your name
and the flower I carry within me.

Run your fingertips along the arch of my
strength.
Words make me cry,
silence hurts more. Either way,
I emerge.

Yes, I have dipped my hands into madness. I have
skied through the cold slopes of self-hatred,
and here I sit –

Emerged,
as you stand in awe of me.

inheritance

I found your absence folded in the linen closet,
tucked inside the scent of old cotton and dust.

It lingers in the rusted hinges
of the door you never got to fix,
in the way the clock still ticks
as if time didn't swallow you whole.

Your voice—
a phantom in the walls,
whispering in the hum of the refrigerator,
in the creak of the floorboards
where you once stood.

I do not know what to do
with all this leftover love.

the hardest truth

I said the words,
but they did not feel like mine.

"My dad is a drug addict."

They sat on my tongue like stones,
heavy, foreign, impossible to swallow.

Then—harder still—

"My mother is an enabler."

The woman who made sure I ate,
who never raised a hand,
who folded herself into the gaps
he left behind.

I could not unwrite the truth
once I had spoken it.

Somehow, it felt like a betrayal.

Somehow, it felt like freedom.

the
haunting

the ghost between us

You are still here,
but only in the way a ghost lingers—
not truly present,
just the echo of something
that once held weight.

The bed remembers your shape,
but you do not sleep here.
The walls remember your voice,
but you do not speak to me.

You have become a name
I no longer say out loud,
a photograph I do not touch,
a presence that feels heavier
in its absence.

How strange,
to grieve the living.

where do you put the love
that has nowhere to go?

I keep finding you
in unexpected places—

In a song I didn't mean to listen to.
In the way the sky looks before rain.
In the empty space
at the dinner table
where no one dares to sit.

Grief is just love
that has nowhere to go.

So I carry it with me.

I tuck it inside my pockets.
I fold it between the pages of books
you would have liked.
I let it press against my ribs
on quiet nights,
whispering your name
so the world does not forget
you were here.

echoes

Your voice still lingers
in the space between heartbeats,
a ghost of a whisper,
a name I don't dare say.

The chair you favored—empty.
The coffee mug—untouched.
Everything I own
is now half of something
that was once whole.

I reach for you in dreams,
but even there,
you are just an echo.

the weight of air

The night swallowed you whole,
left behind only the echo
of your last breath—
a whisper caught in the throat of the wind.

I see you in the dust that lingers
on forgotten picture frames,
in the way the moon bends its light
against the cold windowpane.

The red ball of death floated
just beyond your grasp,
spinning like an eclipsed sun,
too distant to touch,
too close to ignore.

I wonder if you still haunt
the spaces you once filled,
if your fingertips still brush against
the locked doors, the empty chairs,
the spaces where love should have been.

Some nights,
I feel your absence like a weight in my lungs,
a breath I cannot take.

And still,
the world moves forward,
oblivious to the silence
you left behind.

i don't know when it happened

I don't know exactly
when it happened.

Compliments unsaid.
Holidays come and go
without effort.
Hugs out of obligation.

Kids are young and you
blink...

They're grown and
you're lost.

I don't know exactly
when it happened.

Intimacy only for physical
need, not a true
desire for
the old you or
the new you or
the lost you.

Can you hold on?
If you don't know when
it happened?

My mom said I
was pretty.
I was startled by the thought.

Can I be pretty?
sexy?
desirable?

Can you hold on when
you don't know
when it happened?

Or maybe the better question
is
should I?

when i met her

She sat on the edge of a childhood bed,
knees pulled to her chest,
chewing on the silence
like it was something she could swallow whole.

I knelt before her,
older, heavier,
scarred in places she didn't yet know existed.

She did not look up.
But I knew she felt me there,
felt the air shift like a whisper of something
she did not yet believe in.

"You survive this."

Her fingers curled tighter around the hem of her shirt,
knuckles white, breath shallow.
She had learned to make herself small.
She had learned that softness
could be turned into a weapon.

"You survive this."

Her shoulders did not drop,
but her breath—
just for a moment—
stretched deeper into her ribs,
as if she had stolen air
from a future she had not yet seen.

"You grow beyond this room.
Beyond the hands that were too rough,
beyond the voices that told you
who you were allowed to be."

She did not ask how.
She only stared at me,
eyes hollowed by the weight of years
she had not yet lived.

"You will not understand yet,
but you become fire.
And nothing—not him, not them,
not even the ghosts that sleep inside your bones—
can take that from you."

I stood then,
leaving her as she was,
a girl who did not yet believe
but had, at least,
begun to breathe.

fractured time

The past does not stay buried.

It seeps through the cracks,
dripping into quiet moments,
staining the present with echoes
of hands too rough,
words too sharp,
silence too heavy.

Time does not heal.
It only teaches you
to walk carefully
around the broken edges.

splinters

It starts with a crack,
so small you don't notice.
A whisper of pain,
a fleeting shadow.

Then the weight of it settles—
burrowing deep,
a splinter in the soul,
too small to see,
too sharp to ignore.

You learn to live around it,
to carry the wound
like a secret.
But some nights,
when the world is too quiet,
you still feel the sting.

permission

I learned love in clenched fists,
in words that cut deeper
than any wound I could show.

I learned safety in silence,
measured my worth in the weight
of his disappointment.

And still, I carried his name,
his anger,
his voice curling in my throat
like a language I swore
I would never speak.

But the past does not ask
for permission to stay.

the exercise i could not complete

"Picture him sitting across from you,"
the therapist said.

"Tell him what you need to say."

But I could not speak.

I could not see his face,
only the space where it had been,
only the floor where his teeth had fallen.

I could not say
I'm sorry.
I love you.
I miss you.

I could only cry.
And when she asked what I wanted to say,
I whispered,
"I don't know where to look."

i became

Aching and endless desire began our
escapades on rainbows and clouds,
a dream world of happiness where
you were my breath and ~
    I became.

Loneliness crept into our glass home
where every spineless motive created
my reflection and released
stones of fury.
    Dreams were lost ~
I became the pain.

But sleep encrusted eyes can never tell
a lover of the falseness of dreams.
    You are not what I had hoped.

The bruises of neglect and hurtful
words batter against my soul.
In a room that is alone and
dark with the beating of guilt --
possibly the sound of my own heart.
The red ball of desire floating over
fingertips as if dreaming will bring it all back.
　　You are not what I had hoped ~
I became the disgust.

Teeth clenched in the daily fight
toward discovering the reality of mistakes
-- still punishing --
your hands no longer heal me
as my skip crawls away
like the maggot of happiness that manifests into
nothing.
　　You are not what I had hoped ~
I became the failure.

the things he said

You are too much.
You are not enough.
You are the reason
I am like this.

I gathered his words
like stones,
carried them so long
they felt like mine.

Some days,
I still hear his voice
when I look in the mirror.

Some days,
I have to remind myself—
I am not him.
I am not him.

still looking

It's those 12:30 kisses
when the moon shines against your hair
as you switch from dream to dream,
and in the transfer, lean in
to give kisses to my shoulder
as though it wrote notes to my heart.

My body trembles and whispers your
name in response to the owl I
hear questioning me...
    or possibly he questions some grief of his own --
in my selfishness, I hear only
your body's rhythmic twitch against the
sheets.

I got lost once and as I searched
for something in the darkness,
I remembered you and somewhere
in the fog, I found myself.

I laid there remembering.
For, it's in the memories
that my life becomes healed
and shrunk down to a speck
of dust and today becomes
the rainbow that reminds
me of morning's dew.

the echo stops with me

His voice still lingers
in the way I flinch at anger,
in the way my hands hesitate
before reaching for love.

But I refuse to be the echo.
I will not repeat his words
in voices softer than mine.
I will not shape my children
with the same rough edges
that carved me into caution.

I am the silence after the storm,
the first breath of air
after generations of drowning.

The echo stops with me.

some days i want to disappear

Some days, I fantasize about vanishing—
not forever,
not tragically,
just away.

Away from the phone that never stops buzzing,
from the texts that say "Hey, can you—"
before I even open them.

Away from the to-do lists
that are never mine,
from the hands reaching out,
pulling, always pulling.

Somewhere no one needs me.
Where my name is not a request.
Where silence is not a punishment,
but a gift I give myself.

I imagine walking out the door,
leaving the dishes in the sink,
the unread emails,
the plans I didn't make
but somehow became responsible for.

No note.
No explanation.
Just the sound of my own breath
without the weight of expectation
crushing my ribs.

I would never do it.

But some days,
the thought of disappearing
feels lighter than the life
I am expected to carry.

no one saves you

I spent years
waiting for rescue,
for someone to see
the weight I carried
and lift it off my shoulders.

But no one saves you.

Not the man who swore he would.
Not the father who was never whole.
Not the mother who held herself together
with borrowed strength.

You save yourself.

You learn to swim
with lungs full of salt.
You learn to stand
on shaking legs.
You learn that waiting
is another kind of drowning.

And so you rise.
Again.
And again.

Until you no longer remember
how it felt to sink.

the version of me that loved you

Somewhere, she still exists.
The version of me
who loved you.

She is sitting in a quiet room,
waiting for you to see her.
She is twisting herself into something
smaller,
more pleasing,
more digestible.

She does not know yet
that she is wasting away.

She does not know yet
that one day,
I will walk away from her too.

the door i closed

I was raised inside a house
where silence held its breath,
where love was rationed
like something that could run out.

I learned to tiptoe
before I learned to run.
I learned that "I love you"
was sometimes a weapon
instead of a gift.

But I have spent my life
prying open the windows,
letting in the air,
letting in the light,
learning that love
is not meant to be hoarded.

I closed that door behind me.
I will not hand my children
the key.

the
unlearning

the ghosts i carry

Grief does not leave.
It settles in the spaces
between breaths,
between heartbeats,
between the words
I never got to say.

I carry ghosts in my pockets,
folded between the receipts
and the loose change.

They do not ask for much.
Just to be remembered.
Just to be known.

And so I let them stay.
Some things
are not meant to be put down.

the art of leaving

No one teaches you how to leave.
How to walk away from the hands
you once called home.

How to unlearn a name
you spent years answering to.

How to let go of love
that never held you gently.

But I have become an artist of departure.
I have mastered the quiet exit,
the steady hand at the doorknob,
the deep breath before the first step.

And I do not turn back.

Because leaving is not just
walking away—

It is learning that you
were never meant to stay.

penny

I'll see your buck and raise
   you on apathy alone -
after all, isn't that what
   this union is worth?

Tearful cries, deceitful ties,
selfish lies –

You're not worth the penny
I stepped on last night
wearing my favorite Sketchers
and imagining your beautiful
face toppled with seafood.

I dip into the ocean of my
discontent and find you there –
like wet sand in my shoes –
   gritty and hard to pull
   away from.

Don't dare me to see our
bet – I'll always raise you
and win – for I alone am
the Strength you envy as
you cower under

Tearful cries, deceitful ties,
selfish lies –

Raging, rampant, raping desire
got the best of me once as I
toppled along to the wedding
march.
Even then, reality said I felt
you under my heel.
    A penny for my love,
    you say?

I'm worth more than your dreams
on a summer night while the
crocus' sing...

A tune of gospel – softly
and tenderly – you must've
missed that Sunday school
class. You. Mr. Christianity.
Paving your own road to hell
with decorations of consummation
and a love so filled with self-
hatred that it costs more to love
you than love could ever
   be worth.

Shall we wager on the beating
of the hearts or concede
all bets are off? – The
cost is so high, just like the
mountains in California covered
in fluffy whipped cream.
No matter how deep you dig,
all you find is rock.

too tired

I sat in the dim light of grief,
the air thick with the scent of lilies
and whispered condolences.

People came and went,
hands pressed to mine,
tears falling into fabric,
but I was only waiting for one.

Waiting for the man who said he loved me.
Waiting for the man who promised to stand beside me.
Waiting.

It was nearly over when I called.

"Where are you?"

And you—
you were comfortable in your parents' home,
wrapped in routine,
untouched by the kind of loss
that leaves teeth in the floorboards.

"I'm too tired," you said.

Too tired for the weight of death.
Too tired for the sight of my hollowed-out body,
for the silence that stretched between
the casket and the walls.

Too tired for me.

But you found the strength
to appear the next day,
to stand at the funeral,
to let people see you grieving
just enough.

I wonder if you were tired then.

Or if the performance
was worth the effort.

the list

He gave me a blank page
and told me to write two lists.

Body parts I hated.
Body parts I loved.

My pen moved faster
than my mind.
Hate came easy—
hips too wide, ribs too sharp,
thighs that never disappeared enough.
A body I had tried to erase.

But love—
love sat in the corner,
silent, waiting to be noticed.

I hesitated before writing
the curve of my collarbone,
the way my hands could hold things
without breaking them.

"That's a start," he said.

But it didn't feel like one.

the dirty things we do

I mean more than this
I say as I go to have another lunch
against my better senses...

but your eyes are beautiful and your touch
is smooth – and I'm codependent on the
waves of your goodbyes.

I should've left my pants on this time,
but you enticed me to dive right in.
sex is all I know of you
the dirty things we do...

The food was delicious
the passion missing...
I escape my life my love my sanity disappears amidst what
I used to call clarity as I bequeathed my soul to your soul...
and all that mattered to you was the rhythm in my ride.

Next time, I'll glue the buttons and
dismiss you...
you are the fiery pain, freedom's rain, constant reminder that will
believe in Karma when it all comes tumbling down.

'cause sex is all I know of you
the dirty things we do
terrorized, running, raging, rampant love has raped my Self
but won't take my body again...

I left my pants on this time...
the you I know is gone.
Let's face it, the me I knew vanished
in that last moan
as you were still fumbling pitifully to
zip up.

what i was supposed to be

They wanted me quiet.
They wanted me small.
They wanted me to swallow my thoughts
like stones,
let them sink inside me
until I forgot they were mine.

I was supposed to be soft.
Supposed to be agreeable.
Supposed to laugh at the right times,
nod when expected,
live a life
that never made anyone uncomfortable.

But I was never made for that.

I was made to take up space.
To be heard.
To be the kind of wildfire
that does not wait
for permission to burn.

And I am burning.

the body remembers

The body remembers
what the mind has tried to erase.

It wakes in the night, gasping—
not for air,
but for safety.

It flinches at echoes,
sees ghosts in the movement of hands,
carries fear in the muscles,
tucked between the ribs.

The body does not forget.
But maybe, someday,
it will forgive.

the man in the mirror

You have always loved your reflection
more than you have ever loved a person.

More than me.
More than them.
More than the wreckage you left behind.

You polish your image with careful hands,
smoothing the cracks,
rewriting the story,
so no one will see the mess beneath.

You, the misunderstood.
You, the wounded.
You, the man who tried so hard.

I used to lie beside you,
a hollowed-out version of myself,
swallowing sobs in the dark,
while you slept like a man
who had never been cruel a day in his life.

You never noticed.
Or maybe you did—
and simply didn't care.

You ration love like currency,
hand it out when it serves you,
hoard it when it doesn't.

Even your children—
half of you, half of me—
are nothing more than pieces
of your unfinished performance.

You are not a father.
You are an actor.
And I?

I am the woman who left
before the curtain fell.

repetition

I swore I would never choose a man
who spoke venom with his words,
who carved his love into my skin
with the sharp edge of control.

But I mistook familiarity for fate.
I walked into the same fire
with open arms,
believing that maybe this time,
it would not burn.

I handed my children
a story I once begged
to rewrite.

And for that,
I ache in places
no apology can reach.

what i will not pass down

I will not pass down the silence—
the swallowed words, the careful steps,
the fear of love that wounds instead of warms.

I will not teach my children
that love is something to endure.

I will not let them believe
that softness is weakness,
that staying is strength,
that pain is proof of devotion.

I will be the ending
of a story that should have never begun.

she is still in the fire

She wears anger like a second skin,
woven into the lines of her face,
stitched into the spaces
where softness once lived.

She calls it strength.
I know it is armor.

She loves a man who does not see her.
Not really.
His eyes are always looking past her,
through her,
searching for something else.

They fight like fire and gasoline,
like two people who cannot decide
who is the villain
and who is the victim.

Maybe they are both.

Maybe they have forgotten
that love is not supposed to be
a battlefield
where no one ever wins.

I used to think this was love.
The sharp-edged words.
The silence that cuts deeper.
The exhaustion of staying.

But I have unlearned that lesson.

And still,
she stands in the fire,
too close to the flames,
too far from the exit,
believing that if she stays long enough,
it will all burn clean.

what they never told you about survival

They said,
"You made it."

As if that was the end of it.

As if the past does not
wake you up in the night,
clawing its way
through your ribcage.

As if the memories do not
drip into your morning coffee,
press against your skin
like fingerprints
that never fade.

They do not tell you
that survival is not the end.

That it is waking up
and choosing—again and again—
to live with what was left behind.

i have never been soft

I have never been soft.

Not in the way they wanted me to be.
Not in the way that folds into arms
without hesitation,
not in the way that asks
for permission to take up space.

I am sharp edges and wildfire.
I am storms that do not apologize.
I am the kind of woman
who does not break—
only bends, only burns,
only rises again.

And if they call that too much,
let them choke on it.

a war without weapons

They never needed fists.
Not when silence did the job,
when words carved deeper than knives,
when love was a currency
I could never quite afford.

But I do not fight their way.

I do not raise my voice
or sharpen my tongue.
I do not seek vengeance,
only freedom.

Healing is its own rebellion.
Living well is the battle they never saw coming.

And look at me now—
alive.
Whole.
Untouched by the ghosts
who swore they would own me forever.

the things i wish i could tell her

Sweet girl,
one day, you will see
that love is not something
you have to earn.

That hunger is not control.
That kindness should not
cost you everything.

That you do not have to
set yourself on fire
just to keep someone else warm.

One day,
you will know your worth.
And when you do,
you will never let someone
take it from you again.

the
becoming

unapologetic

I have made myself small
so men could feel bigger.
I have swallowed my voice
so theirs could echo louder.

I have starved myself,
shrunk my body,
softened my edges,
erased my hunger,
as if disappearing
was the price of being loved.

No more.

No more shrinking
to fit inside their comfort.
No more laughing
at jokes that taste like rust.
No more bowing
so they don't feel beneath me.

I was never meant to be small.
I was never meant to be quiet.
I was never meant to apologize
for the space I take up.

So listen—
I will not whisper.
I will not bend.
I will not giggle to make you feel
like more of a man.

I am a force.
A wildfire.
A storm that does not ask
permission to shake the ground.

And if you fear me,
good.

Because you should.

do not call me small

Do not call me small.
Do not mistake my quiet for compliance,
my softness for submission,
my kindness for permission
to take what is not yours.

I am not delicate.
I am not breakable.
I am not here to be handled gently,
like something meant to be put back
where you found it.

I have been burning for years.

Burning my way out of cages
I did not build.
Burning through the lies
I once believed.
Burning down the idea
that I should make myself less
so you can feel like more.

I do not shrink.
I do not bow.
I do not giggle when I want to roar.

So if my fire scorches you,
step back.
If my voice unsettles you,
cover your ears.
If my presence makes you tremble,
then tremble.

I am not here to be small enough
for you to hold.

I am here to take up space
until the walls shake.

sunrise

I'm stepping to your heart asking it to love me,
   with all my imperfections...
in each, there is beauty and a desire
   so deep for you that sometimes
it's hard to breathe without
crying.

Forgive the confusion in me as I forgive the apathy in you.
Remember all those times when
   we couldn't tell where your arm ended
and my arm began, wrapped in the moment
   of lust and love and every
sunrise we've ever felt on our faces.

a woman like me

A woman like me
is not meant to be quiet.
Not meant to sit pretty,
to be polite,
to make herself smaller
so someone else can feel tall.

A woman like me
does not soften her voice
for fragile egos,
does not apologize for her fire,
does not ask permission
to exist loudly.

A woman like me
will shake the ground you stand on
and dare you to hold steady.

the weight of motherhood

I do not know where she went—
the girl I was before they called me mother.

She was here, once,
laughing too loudly,
sleeping without guilt,
dancing without reason.

Now, she is buried beneath
lunchboxes and late nights,
behind hands that soothe,
behind eyes that scan for danger
before it comes.

I love them more than breath,
more than my own skin,
but sometimes,
I miss the girl
who did not belong to anyone.

soft love

I did not know
love could be quiet.

That it could arrive
like a slow sunrise,
creeping in without demand,
without urgency.

Love once felt like fire,
like hunger,
like an ache that could never be filled.

But this—
this is different.

This is safety.
This is steady hands.
This is love that does not ask me
to prove my worth.

becoming

I have spent years shedding skins,
each one a past version of me.
The girl who swallowed her words,
the woman who lived in shadows,
the dreamer who forgot to dream.

I am finding her again,
the one who dances barefoot,
who laughs too loud,
who speaks her truth
even when her voice shakes.

I am still becoming.

twitch

Remember that time I was sick?
When we were curled into each other...
You leaned into my ear and whispered,
"Do you want to orgasm?"

As soon as I said yes,
the fever blended with the passion
and everything else was forgotten.

You used your shirt to mute
my moans but I'd forgotten
where I was.
All I could focus on was
your strong hands and
my rhythmic twitch.

the kind of woman i have become

I am not the woman
I once was.

She was quiet.
She was careful.
She was trying so hard
to be what everyone else needed.

But I have burned
through every version of me
that was not real.

And now—
now I am the woman
who does not ask for permission,
who does not shrink,
who does not fear the sound
of her own voice.

I am the kind of woman
who walks away when love is not real.
Who does not bow to the past.
Who builds herself
from the ashes of everything
that tried to break her.

set me on fire

Do not love me softly.
Do not ask me to be quiet,
to be still,
to be anything less
than wildfire.

I have spent too many years
burning in silence,
turning my heat inward,
melting myself down
to fit inside hands
that never deserved to hold me.

No more.

If you cannot handle the fire,
do not step into my arms.

you wouldn't recognize me now

You wouldn't recognize me now.

Not with the way I stand,
spine straight,
chin high,
heart still beating
after everything.

Not with the way my name
is no longer a whisper,
but a full-bodied roar
that does not tremble
when spoken aloud.

Not with the way
I no longer flinch,
no longer shrink,
no longer wait
for someone else to choose me.

I am already chosen.
I chose myself.

And you—
you are nothing more
than a shadow
at my back.

not a good girl

I have been called many things—

Too much.
Too loud.
Too angry.
Too proud.

I have been told to be softer.
To be smaller.
To be more delicate.

To be what they call
"a good girl."

But I was not made to be good.

I was made to be free.

the woman who disappeared

She wakes before the sun,
washes yesterday from her skin,
drinks coffee that never touches her bones.

She moves through the day
like a ghost in her own body.
Get up.
Work.
Eat.
Wash the dishes.
Go to bed.
Repeat.

She has learned to live in echoes,
in lists and obligations,
in the weight of doing
without remembering
why.

There was a time she loved things.

The way words felt against her fingertips,
the way the sky looked right before a storm,
the way laughter could shake
something loose inside her ribs.

But now—
she is only function.
Only necessity.
Only motion without memory.

She stares at her own reflection
and wonders when she stopped
being a person
and became a task to complete.

the body keeps it all

I have worn exhaustion like armor,
carried stress between my shoulder blades
until my body bowed beneath it.

I have clenched my jaw through words
I did not speak,
held my breath through moments
I did not want to live.

My body remembers
what my mind tries to erase.

But healing looks like
unclenching my fists,
uncurling my spine,
letting my own name sit
softly in my mouth
without apology.

learning softness

I am learning
that healing is not a war
I must win,
but a garden
I must tend.

Softness grows where scars once lived.
Peace lingers in the spaces
where I once held my breath.

I do not flinch at my own reflection anymore.
I do not brace for impact
where there is no battle.

I am learning
how to be gentle with myself.

the
rising

the second life

The first life was for surviving.
For enduring.
For becoming what was needed,
even if it meant losing myself.

But this—
this is my second life.

This is the life
where I do not shrink,
where I do not apologize,
where I do not bleed myself dry
to quench another's thirst.

I have already died once—
in silence, in surrender,
in the quiet disappearance of self.

This time,
I will not go so easily.

inheritance of light

My father taught me how to break,
how to fold into myself like paper—
silent, small, unseen.

But I have learned the language of light.

I open my hands,
and the sun finds me.

I open my mouth,
and my voice sings its way home.

I was not meant to be dimmed.

unfinished

I trace my name into your skin,
each letter dissolving into heat.
You breathe me in—
a whisper, a promise,
a fever with no cure.

Fingertips hesitate, then surrender.
We speak in tongues of longing,
a silent language written
in the arch of my back,
the curve of your hand.

The night is a canvas,
we paint in shadows,
unfinished strokes of want
never meant to dry.

between the breaths

Your name lingers between my breaths,
a quiet confession
woven into the silence.

Your hands, a slow-burning fuse—
tracing stories against my skin,
rewriting the past with each touch.

I dissolve beneath you,
a whispered prayer
on the altar of your mouth.

And still,
it is never enough.

hunger

You kiss me like the ocean swallows the shore—
hungry, relentless,
pulling me under before I remember how to breathe.

Your hands write poems along my skin,
each touch a stanza,
each sigh an unfinished verse
drifting between our lips.

I surrender to the tide,
to the taste of salt and sin,
to the gravity of longing
that bends me toward you,
again and again.

unbecoming

I have spent years unraveling,
peeling away layers that were never mine to wear.

The good girl. The quiet wife.
The mother who forgets herself
in the needs of others.

I set fire to the versions of me
that no longer fit,
watch the embers curl into the sky.

Somewhere in the ashes,
I find her—
the woman I was always meant to be.

they are not mine

I carried them beneath my ribs,
woven into the rhythm of my pulse,
as if they were mine
to keep.

I traced the curves of their faces,
mapped futures upon their foreheads,
whispered stories into the soft
folds of their sleep—
believing I could shape the tide
with my hands.

But the wind does not ask
where it may blow.
The river does not seek permission
before carving new paths.

And they—
they are not mine,
though my entire heart
is pulled into their bodies,
a tide that rises and falls
with every step they take away from me.

I watch them unfold,
not as I dreamed,
but as they are—
wild and uncontainable,
choosing roads I did not name,
singing songs I do not know.

It is both grief and grace
to love something
that was never meant to stay.

And so, I stand on the shore,
hands open,
watching them drift into the world,
knowing the only thing I was ever meant to do
was love them
as they go.

fingertip prayers

Your hands move like scripture—
a whispered psalm against my skin,
each fingertip a prayer
that makes my body bow.

I answer in exhales,
in the trembling hush of surrender,
in the way my pulse confesses
everything my lips do not say.

We are devout in our worship,
sinners in our longing,
kneeling only to each other
in the midnight quiet.

the parts i keep

I no longer know
where I end
and they begin.

Motherhood reshaped me,
took my edges,
smoothed them into hands
made for holding,
a heart made for breaking
a thousand times over.

But there are parts of me
I still keep—
the dreamer,
the girl who once ran barefoot,
the woman who still believes
she is more than what she gives away.

i did not die with it

There are things that should have broken me.
Things that should have buried me.

Things I should not have crawled out of.

But look at me—
standing,
breathing,
building something new
from the rubble they left behind.

I did not die with it.

And that is enough revenge
for a lifetime.

breaking the cycle

I once thought healing
was a moment—
a single act of courage,
a door slammed shut
on the past.

But healing is the choice
to walk away every day,
to unlearn the love
that looked like fear,
to show my children
a world where love
does not leave bruises
on the soul.

It is not easy
to break a cycle
that has been spinning
for generations.

But I would rather
be the one to bleed
than the one
who makes them suffer.

becoming the phoenix

I have burned before,
turned to ash beneath hands
that never learned how to hold.

I have crumbled,
disappeared into dust
under the weight of my past.

But I have also risen—
flames licking at my heels,
smoke curling in my lungs,
reborn from the embers
of who I used to be.

I am the fire now.

i will not be the quiet woman

I will not be the quiet woman.
The one who nods.
The one who swallows her voice
like it was never hers to keep.

I will not be the woman
who dims herself
so someone else can shine,
who softens her edges
so the world is not uncomfortable
with her fire.

I have burned before.
And I will burn again.

But I will not
go quietly.

i found myself in ireland

I followed the mist to the edges of cliffs,
where the world dropped away
but I did not.

The wind carried whispers
of a woman I once knew,
her voice tangled in the tall grass,
her laughter pressed into cobblestone streets
worn smooth by centuries of footsteps.

I dipped my hands into the rain
and washed away the weight
of every version of me
that was never mine to carry.

The hills stretched wide,
a green so wild it felt like breathing
for the first time.
And I thought—
perhaps I have been asleep until now.

Perhaps I was always meant
to stand here,
feet sinking into the damp earth,
arms open to the salted wind,
learning that I do not have to belong
to anyone
to belong to myself.

Ireland did not give me answers.
It did not fill my empty spaces.
But it reminded me
that I have always been whole—

I just needed to see myself
from the top of a cliff,
with nothing but sky ahead,
and know that I was never lost.

the kind of love
that does not hurt

This love does not feel like hunger.
It does not leave me starving,
waiting to be fed.

This love does not demand my silence.
It does not shrink me down
until I fit inside his shadow.

This love is gentle hands,
soft words,
a quiet place to land.

This love is warmth without fire,
safety without sacrifice,
a love that does not
ask me to bleed to prove it is real.

what they don't tell
you about survival

They will call you strong.
They will marvel at your resilience,
at the way you stitched yourself back together
without crying out.

But they will not ask
what it cost you.

They will not ask about the nights
you held your breath in the dark,
about the weight in your chest
that still has not lifted.

They will not see the parts of you
that are still missing,
the pieces you had to leave behind
just to make it out alive.

Survival is not a medal.
It is a scar.

scars like constellations

There was a time I believed
I would not survive this body,
this skin that betrayed me,
this heart that cracked like porcelain.

But look at me now—
stitched together with fire,
wearing my bruises like war paint,
scars like constellations,
mapping the journey back to myself.

I am no longer afraid
of my own reflection.

about the author

Cristie Robbins is a poet and writer whose work explores grief, trauma, resilience, and healing. Through raw and evocative verse, she captures the intricacies of loss, the echoes of the past, and the strength required to rise again. Her writing is a testament to survival and self-discovery, offering solace to those who have walked similar paths.

When she is not writing, Cristie is passionate about mental wellness and personal growth, helping others navigate their own journeys toward healing. She believes that every scar tells a story, and within those stories, we find our power.

www.ingramcontent.com/pod-product-compliance
Lightning Source LLC
Chambersburg PA
CBHW020419150626
46554CB00014B/2091